COMBATTING BULLYING AT WORK

A widespread problem
in the modern workplace

Written by Benjamin Fléron
Translated by Rebecca Neal

Coaching 50MINUTES.com

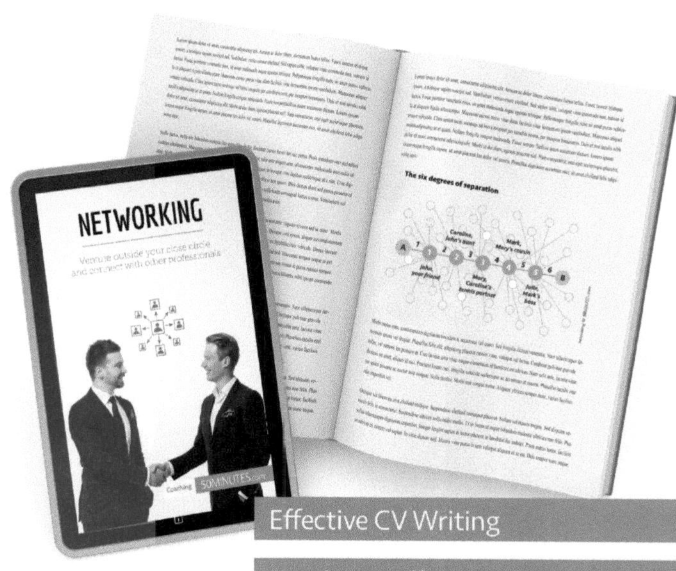

50MINUTES.com

PROPEL
YOUR BUSINESS FORWARD!

NETWORKING
Venture outside your close circle
and connect with other professionals

Effective CV Writing

Resolving Office Conflict

Boost Your Concentration

Find Your Work-Life Balance

www.50minutes.com

COMBATTING BULLYING AT WORK

- **Problem:** how can you recognise bullying at work, guard against it and respond effectively if the need arises?
- **Uses:** as bullying is sadly a common occurrence in the world of work, it is useful to be able to forestall, identify and combat it.
- **Professional context:** work psychology, employment law, human resources.
- **FAQs:**
  - How can I know for certain whether I am being bullied?
  - How can I guard against bullying and defend myself if it happens to me?
  - What should I do if I realise that one of my colleagues is being bullied?
  - What should I do if a loved one tells me that they are being bullied?
  - What is mobbing?
  - Can bullying be organised?
  - What are the risks associated with reporting

bullying?
  ◦ What about harassment?

You would be forgiven for thinking that insults, mockery, ostracism and public humiliation had been left behind on the playground and have no place in the world of work. However, these demeaning behaviours, which seek to rob victims of their dignity, are a fact of life for many workers. Anyone can be a victim of bullying, from freelancers to civil servants and from entry-level employees to senior managers, and this mistreatment can have serious consequences. But what can we do about it?

Bullying is a problem that knows no borders, and you may already be familiar with it. Maybe, like most people, you have simply heard it talked about on TV or in conversations, or perhaps it has affected you indirectly if a loved one or colleague has been a victim. Alternatively, you may be acutely aware of this situation if you have previously experienced it or are currently living with it.

Whatever your relationship with bullying, and even if you think it has nothing to do with you, it is imperative that you avoid dismissing it out of hand and take steps to defend yourself against it. Whether you are an employee or a company owner, you are a potential victim of bullying, and failing to give this problem the attention it requires could have disastrous consequences, both for you and for your company.

BULLYING: THE BASICS

AN INDIVIDUAL PROBLEM WITH FAR-REACHING CONSEQUENCES

While there is no legal definition of bullying in the workplace, Acas, which provides support and advice for workers and employers, defines it as "offensive, intimidating, malicious or insulting behaviour, an abuse or misuse of power through means that undermine, humiliate, denigrate or injure the person being bullied" which happens "repeatedly and persistently over time" (cited in Landau 2017).

The bully's arsenal is packed with weapons that they can use against their unfortunate target, and they do not shy away from using them. They make unsparing use of cruel words, attempts to humiliate, inappropriate behaviours and malicious emails to break the spirit of their victim, who does not understand what is happening to them and is at a loss to deal with the situation.

Victims are typically wholly unprepared to deal

with this onslaught of cruelty, and by the time they are ready to respond it is often too late: by this time, events may have spiralled out of their control, leaving them unsure how to escape the situation and pushing them deeper into trouble. The physical and emotional effects of bullying can be devastating: they include nervous disorders, sleep disturbances, loss of appetite, stomach ulcers, sadness, anger and feelings of powerlessness or worthlessness. Bullying can also lead to serious mental health problems such as depression, burnout, mental breakdowns and even suicide in extreme cases.

The situation also has consequences for the company that employs the bully and their victim: time lost through frequent sick days, underhanded behaviour that causes delays in work or stops it from being completed, a constantly worsening atmosphere at work, one person who is always afraid and another whose energy is devoted to scheming rather than to their work, and so on. This obviously diminishes the company's productivity, and can even seriously harm its image if the media gets wind of the situation.

MYTHS AND MISCONCEPTIONS

When it comes to bullying, and workplace bullying in particular, some myths seem to be accepted as fact, and they may allow many bullies to go undetected and remain above suspicion even as they make their victims' lives a misery.

Even today, many people do not see themselves as the victims of a bona fide bully for the (false) reason that their tormentor does not match up to their mental image of a bully. For the same reason, many people do not believe some victims, who are left feeling desperate and ignored. Consequently, it is vital to begin by clearing up some of the myths that still circulate about bullying and shining a light on the truth.

Bullies are not necessarily their victims' superiors

This is undoubtedly the most widespread misconception about workplace bullying and, consequently, the most frequent mistake people make. We can all imagine an irate boss screaming at their terrified subordinate, but the reality is often completely different.

While it is true that "downward bullying" (as illustrated in our previous example) is the most common type of workplace bullying, "horizontal bullying", between colleagues on the same level, can also take place.

More surprising, and also rarer, is "upward bullying". For example, employees who are unhappy about the dismissal of a popular supervisor, which they had no say in, may turn against their new manager, who they see as something of a usurper.

Although bullying is intrinsically linked to power dynamics and always has a dominant and a dominated party, these positions do not necessarily reflect the official hierarchy.

Bullies are not all men

Studies on bullying have shown that the majority of bullies are men, but this is not always the case: woman are just as capable of bullying, and their victims may be men. It is already difficult for people to admit that they are being bullied and to open up to other people about it, and this is especially the case for men who are being bullied by a woman, as they may be afraid of being ridiculed, of not being believed or of inspiring pity in their male peers.

Bullies are not easily identifiable monsters

You may be thinking that you would know a bully if you saw one, or that the person who is making your life a misery cannot possibly be a bully, because if they were you would not be the only person to have problems with them.

This is one of the cruxes of the problem: bullies often do not appear to be monsters, and may be widely seen as completely normal. In fact, bullies do not attack everyone indiscriminately, but select a single target for their mistreatment and cruelty.

Furthermore, bullies make sure that they operate discreetly in order to evade suspicion and, above all, to make people think that their victim is paranoid and is imagining the persecution they are experiencing. For example, constant criticisms and hurtful remarks will not be delivered in a threatening or unpleasant tone, but slipped subtly into the conversation, disguised as complements or said with a smile, as though they should not be taken seriously.

Contrary to popular belief, the truth is that many bullies are very personable and likeable to people who are not subject to their attacks on a daily basis.

Victims of bullying are not naturally fragile

We often tend to think of the victims of bullying as naturally fragile people who have been in similar situations throughout their lives (punchbags in the playground, outcasts within their family, and so on). However, nothing could be further from the truth. The myth of the weak, timid, fearful victim who more or less asks for the mistreatment they receive has gone on for long enough and needs to be laid to rest. We are all potential victims of bullying, regardless of our personality and character. No matter how strong, intelligent or highly educated we are, we are still human and will live though our share of difficult times. There are plenty of events that we cannot avoid and that will inevitably weaken us: when we experience a break-up, the loss of a loved one, illness, or even just an event that we are not used to (such as entering the job market), we need time to adapt. Lowering your guard, no matter how briefly, allows the bully to step into the breach and silently drag you down.

MISCONCEPTIONS ABOUT BULLYING: SUMMARY

- Bullies:
  - are not always above their victims in the professional hierarchy;
  - are not always men;
  - are not necessarily easy to identify.

- Anyone can be a victim of bullying.

AM I BEING BULLIED?

Although this may seem strange, it is not always easy to be completely sure that you are being bullied at work. Is the colleague who dislikes you and seems to take a kind of twisted pleasure in taking their time to send you the information you desperately need bullying you? What about the demanding manager who is quick to raise his voice when he is unhappy with your work? Or your boss, who makes fun of you in front of everyone every time you slip up? Is he just a joker with a questionable sense of humour, or something more sinister?

Misunderstandings, tensions and harsh disapproval are common occurrences in the world of work, which means that it can be difficult to tell the difference between behaviour resulting from a personality clash and bullying. Fortunately, although bullying can take many forms, there are some clear-cut signs that exist in most cases and that will allow you to know for certain whether or not you are being bullied.

The actions are repeated over an extended period of time

Heated discussions, hurtful comments, damaging rumours and cheap shots are unfortunately frequent in the world of work, especially if the sector you work in is highly competitive and encourages rivalry between colleagues.

- Your boss is in a particularly bad mood and be-

rates you about the quality of your work, when you do not think that you have done anything wrong.
- A colleague who is normally warm and friendly is struggling with some personal problems and all of a sudden becomes distant and responds coolly when you try to talk to them.
- A colleague who has worked well with you until now is angling for a promotion, so they report all your mistakes, no matter how trivial, to your supervisor.

While these situations may be unpleasant, they are a normal part of working life and should not be classed as bullying if they only happen occasionally. For these incidents to count as bullying, they should recur regularly over the course of several months.

The attacks are personal, targeted and gratuitous

The bully does not have a problem with your work, but with you personally. Consequently, their nastiness and constant attacks often have nothing to do with the quality of your work, but rather target you as a person: laughing at your appearance, mocking your accent or way of speaking, making racist or sexist jokes, doing demeaning impressions of you, making fun of your private life, and so on. Nothing is off limits, and the bully may attack you from a variety of angles.

The bully tries to physically and/or psychologically isolate you

Most bullies are exceptionally skilled at this, and go about it in several different ways. For example, some people are very good at spreading rumours while making it seem like they had nothing to do with them, and over time these slanderous comments are simply accepted as fact by the rest of your coworkers. If your colleagues stop trusting you and side with the bully, you will find yourself ostracised.

If the bully stays in control of themselves in all situations while constantly needling their victim until they snap, they will attract the sympathy of outside observers, who do not notice their efforts to undermine the other person but cannot fail to see the victim's hostile reaction.

When the victim is isolated, has no support and feels that they have been abandoned, they are much more vulnerable and sensitive to attacks. If the victim is unlucky enough to be their tormentor's subordinate, the bully can also try to physically separate them from their colleagues, for example by giving them tasks that require them to be somewhere else, away from their coworkers, or by giving them a new, completely isolated place to work.

The bully tries to stop you from doing your work

Bullies will not stop at continually putting their victims down, but will also try to stop them from carrying out their work effectively. They have a wide range of ways of doing this, and will vary their approach depending on their relationship with their target.

- If they are their supervisor, they can put them in charge of a poorly defined project and constantly give them contradictory orders and instructions.
- They can also give their subordinate tasks that they are not qualified for, or tasks that are

demeaning in view of their qualifications and level of education: for example, a person with multiple degrees could be asked to make coffee or do the photocopying, while an untrained entry-level employee could be tasked with working on extremely complex specialised projects.
- The bully could also keep essential information to themselves by only passing on part of it to their victim or giving it to them at the last moment in order to cause problems for them or to be able to reprimand them for finishing the work late.

IDENTIFYING BULLYING: SUMMARY

- Repeated attacks over an extended period of time.
- Personal attacks rather than constructive criticism of the victim's work.
- Attacks on a single person, who ends up isolated.
- Attacks which aim to sabotage the victim's work.

EMPLOYERS: PREVENTION IS BETTER THAN CURE

Although this statement may seem to be something of a cliché, that does not make it any less true in the situation at hand. Without even going into cases which could have been prevented in advance, many cases could have been resolved before they escalated if employers had paid greater attention to what was going on and acted more responsibly.

By being proactive and taking a strong stance early on, you can guard against a good deal of misconduct. The majority of the most common pitfalls when it comes to dealing with bullying at work can be avoided by respecting the basic principles outlined below.

Fair, decent working conditions

Basic equipment problems like faulty lighting, broken heating, faded walls, too few computers and outdated IT systems will have an impact on your employees' mood and damage the working environment. When they think that not everyone is in the same boat and that some people have better working conditions than others, feelings of injustice and unfairness may emerge and lead to serious problems in relationships between colleagues. These problems may in turn give rise to bullying.

Effective information flows

To avoid misunderstandings between your employees, not only must the information they are given be clear and precise, but it must circulate appropriately and reach all staff at the same time. Vague instructions often give rise to different, contradictory interpretations and to pointless tensions. To prevent these problems, ensure complete transparency and effective information flows.

Fair distribution of tasks

Make sure you do not overload some of your employees while others have next to nothing to do, as this will sap everyone's morale. The overworked employees will feel that they are being treated unfairly and are likely to resent the colleagues who are not pulling their weight, while the underworked staff members will feel useless at best, and completely undervalued at worst. It is essential that everybody takes on their share of the work and that each person's tasks are appropriate for their skills and their role.

A calm working environment

If you absolutely have to reprimand one of your employees, and at the same time you want to congratulate one of their direct colleagues on the quality of their work, have the presence of mind to take each of them aside privately rather than airing your views on their work in front of everybody. Similarly, try to avoid giving out performance bonuses and do not give in to the temptation to hand out "employee of the month" awards, as these will only inspire jealousy between colleagues. Always remember that your staff members are supposed to be teammates, not rivals.

EMPLOYER ACTION: SUMMARY

- Ensure fair, decent working conditions.
- Ensure effective information flows.

- Make sure that tasks are divided fairly.
- Do not encourage competition between colleagues.

I AM BEING BULLIED AT WORK. WHAT CAN I DO?

If, after taking the time to think over the facts, you have come to the conclusion that you are being bullied at work, do not panic, as the situation is far from hopeless. You can always flee your tormentor, but there are also other, far less extreme, ways of resolving things. Before taking a step from which there is no going back, and which will leave your tormentor unpunished and free to start again with a new target, take the time to consider each of the following solutions.

Tell someone about it

Many victims of bullying are too afraid to talk about it and allow the situation to get worse until it is beyond fixing. Do not be one of them!

As we have already seen, bullies are skilled at isolating their victims and convincing them that they are alone, that they have been abandoned by everybody, and that nobody is going to help them. Obviously, this is in their best interests: isolation makes people fragile and vulnerable, whereas support and attention give them strength. Some bullies are so cunning that they even make their victims wonder whether their behaviour was justified: "Maybe I deserved it. Is it even really bullying? Maybe I'm imagining the whole thing". If you find yourself having these thoughts, it is essential that you talk to some-body: no matter how you may feel, you are not alone.

Gather physical evidence

Bullying is not always easy to prove, and all

too often it comes down to one person's word against another's. While the support and eyewitness accounts of your colleagues can help you to prove that what you are saying is true, it would be risky to rely too much on them, as they may stay silent out of fear for their jobs or even side with your bully if they believe them over you. They may also be completely oblivious to the bullying that is happening right in front of them.

The best thing to do is therefore to gather as much physical evidence as possible and to hold on to it for when you need it. Keep everything (derogatory emails, abusive texts, contradictory memos, vague or ambiguous instructions, information sent at the last minute followed by reprimands for working too slowly), as it can all support your case. If possible, try to keep a diary at home and away from prying eyes, in which you make a note of every insulting comment and instance of unreasonable behaviour.

Keep your cool

By making your life a living hell, the bully is trying to get you to fly off the handle. Do not give them the satisfaction, and remain outwardly indifferent as they attack you. You should make it seem that their actions do not affect you, but slide off you like water off a duck's back. For example, you could respond to their unpleasant remarks with humour. Do not forget that all bullies need a victim, and that there are no victims without aggression. If you refuse to consider their behaviour as an attack, you are refusing to be a victim, which in turn deprives the bully of their power over you.

Furthermore, do not forget that, generally speaking, your bully will always be even-tempered and will never raise their voice. By passing insulting, demeaning comments off as jokes, they avoid drawing attention to themselves and fool everyone into thinking that they are no different from anyone else. Respond to them in the same joking tone, or tell them calmly but firmly that they have overstepped the mark and you are not going to stand for it. If you do not remain just as unflappable as them and hit back hard at one of their comments, the bully will be quick to play the victim and turn everyone else against you by painting you as paranoid and overly suspicious. Keeping your cool will prevent you from being seen as the bad guy and essentially digging your own grave.

Confront the bully

Before you get to the point where you are taking regular sick days and considering resigning to avoid your bully's constant attacks, think about confronting them and trying to come to some sort of understanding. If possible, arrange a meeting with them and a HR representative and use it to try and clear up the situation. Show them that you are not going to tolerate their behaviour and are prepared to stand up for yourself, and may even take legal action if the situation calls for it. This may force them to change their behaviour towards you.

TOP TIPS

- **Be proactive.** Do not wait until you are being bullied to take action; instead, make the first move and guard against it as much as possible. Identify your company's shortcomings when it comes to dealing with bullying, whether they are structural (infrastructure or equipment issues, poor information flows, unfair distribution of tasks, and so on) or human (lack of preventative measures, poor atmosphere, competitive environment, and so on), and either tell somebody else or take the necessary steps yourself if it is in your power to do so.
- **Work on your self-esteem.** Like sharks drawn to the scent of blood, bullies are good at sensing weakness and know how to hit people where it hurts. Remember that, just as nobody is perfect, nobody is completely worthless. Recognise your good points and learn to live with your flaws, as this will leave potential bullies with nothing to latch onto.
- **Refuse to be a victim.** Do not play the bully's game by simply accepting this role. Stand firm,

set clear limits on the behaviour you will and will not tolerate, and do not let anybody flout them. Know your rights as a worker and stand up for them if you have to.

- **Do not lose sight of the role you were hired for and do not hesitate to ask your manager to clarify it if need be.** This will help you to determine what is a part of your role and what is suited to your skills, and, conversely, what is not your responsibility. If your position is clearly defined, it will be more difficult to give you tasks that are not your responsibility or that you are not qualified for.
- **Talk to someone.** Silence is the bully's best friend, so speak up about what they are doing to you. Every time they make an inappropriate comment, repeat it out loud in an even tone and without adding anything. Since their aim in repeating their remarks is to gradually convince the people around you that they are true, adopt the same approach: every time they lay into you, you can say in a joking way to the people around you that they seem to have something against you personally. When this idea takes root in your colleagues' minds, they will be more likely to pick up on the bul-

ly's behaviour. Finally, if you are too afraid to talk about it openly, or if you think that the people around you are against you and that nobody will believe you, sharing your pain anonymously on the internet could be a good solution. You will soon realise that you are not alone and that other people are going through the same ordeal as you, which will in turn help you to understand that there is every reason to tell someone about your situation, and that you are the victim rather than the guilty party.

FAQS

HOW CAN I KNOW FOR CERTAIN WHETHER I AM BEING BULLIED?

Although it is not always easy to know whether you are being targeted by a bully, some signs are present in most cases and will give you a good indication. A situation is generally classed as workplace bullying if it involves:

- repeated incidents (at least one per week) over an extended period of time (several months);
- personal, targeted attacks that have nothing to do with work, such as making fun of a person's appearance, intelligence or personality, doing demeaning impersonations of them, and spreading rumours about their private life;
- premeditated attempts to stop the victim from doing their work correctly by putting excessive pressure on them, giving them faulty equipment or material, giving vague or contradictory instructions, withholding information, assigning the victims tasks which do not correspond with their role or for which they are

over- or underqualified, and so on;

- isolation and sidelining (inventing rumours with the aim of ostracising the victim, accusing them of being paranoid or overreacting if they hit back, giving them tasks to do alone or in an isolated workspace).

HOW CAN I GUARD AGAINST BULLYING AND DEFEND MYSELF IF IT HAPPENS TO ME?

- Stand up for yourself: work on your self-esteem, pay attention to your strong points and accept your flaws. Know your rights and do not be afraid to stand up for them.
- Tell someone: this could mean family, friends or a HR representative at work.
- Keep your cool: remain impassive and unflappable. Take away the bully's power by refusing to be a victim.
- Gather evidence: keep emails, texts, memos and notes that could prove that you are being bullied. Keep a diary of the bully's behaviour in case you open formal proceedings against them.
- Confront the bully, in the presence of a HR

representative: discuss their behaviour and try to come to an amicable solution to the problem. Take legal action against them if nothing changes.

WHAT SHOULD I DO IF I REALISE THAT ONE OF MY COLLEAGUES IS BEING BULLIED?

If you think that one of your colleagues is being bullied, there are many steps you can take, without it seeming like you are meddling in issues that do not concern you.

- Do not make the bully's work any easier: challenge their slanderous comments and refute any false allegations, even if the rest of your coworkers are on their side.
- Objectively draw attention to any unreasonable behaviour and anything that looks like bullying. This could include contradictory orders, vague instructions, unfair distribution of tasks, and so on.
- If the situation seems to be getting worse, inform HR.

WHAT SHOULD I DO IF A LOVED ONE TELLS ME THAT THEY ARE BEING BULLIED?

The best thing you can do in this situation is support the victim: listen to them, believe them, give them advice, tell them about their rights, help them to take effective action and support them through it.

WHAT IS MOBBING?

This term is sometimes used to refer to group bullying, where several people gang up on a single victim. In the workplace, a bully may enlist other colleagues to exclude or harass their unfortunate target, leaving them feeling even more isolated and alone.

CAN BULLYING BE ORGANISED?

Unfortunately, sometimes bullying can even be planned by the company itself. By pushing one or more employees to resign, it can get out of paying them severance money and can avoid damaging its image by being seen to dismiss staff unfairly.

WHAT ARE THE RISKS ASSOCIATED WITH REPORTING BULLYING?

In the UK, employees cannot be dismissed for exposing wrongdoing in the workplace, which could include making bullying and mistreatment public. Similarly, you may be able to take legal action in cases of constructive dismissal, meaning cases when your employer's conduct forces you to leave you job. This conduct could include forcing you to accept unreasonable changes to how you work (which may arise if you are being bullied by a superior) or allowing other employees to harass or bully you.

WHAT ABOUT HARASSMENT?

While bullying itself is not against the law in the UK, harassment is. This refers to hostile behaviour based on factors such as age, sex, sexual orientation, race, religion and disability. According to the Equality Act 2010, harassment is a form of unlawful discrimination and involves "unwanted or unwelcome behaviour" which is either intended to or has the effect of "violating your dignity or creating an intimidating, hostile, degrading, humiliating or offensive environ-ment" (Citizens Advice). Harassment can take the form of unwanted comments, threats or abuse, offensive comments on social media and pranks, among others. According to the Act, your employer has a duty to ensure that you are not harassed by your colleagues at work; if they fail in this duty, you can make a claim against both the colleague who is harassing you and the company in an employment tribunal.

OVER TO YOU

IMPROVE YOUR WORK ENVIRONMENT

If you are running a company and want to make sure that your business is not a breeding ground for bullying, use the following checklist to take targeted action and give yourself the best possible chance of creating a healthy work environment.

Work environment

OBSERVATIONS		ACTIONS
Heating/air conditioning work properly	Yes/No	
Sufficient quantities of good-quality office equipment	Yes/No	
Office equipment shared out fairly	Yes/No	
Noncompetitive work environment	Yes/No	
Effective information flows	Yes/No	
Dialogue within the company encouraged	Yes/No	
Team building activities	Yes/No	
Clear instructions for all tasks	Yes/No	
Tasks shared out fairly	Yes/No	
Regular individual feedback	Yes/No	
...	...	

IDENTIFY BULLYING

If you are having doubts or feel unsure whether or not a particular situation constitutes bullying, use the checklist below to draw your own conclusions.

Bullying checklist

IN CASES OF BULLYING, THE ACTIONS:	OBSERVATION
take place repeatedly over an extended period of time	Yes/No
are often directed at the same person	Yes/No
physically and/or psychologically isolate the victim	Yes/No
aim to personally humiliate the victim	Yes/No
do not provide constructive criticism of the person's work, but belittle them personally	Yes/No
slow down and/or disrupt work	Yes/No
are carried out by an employee who is otherwise well-liked within the company	Yes/No
...	...

TAKE ACTION AGAINST BULLYING

If you are sure that the situation you are dealing with is really bullying, develop a multi-step plan of action by following the "top tips" outlined previously. This will give you the tools you need (or the tools the victim needs, if you are just a witness) to stop the bully from getting away with it.

We want to hear from you!
Leave a comment on your online library
and share your favourite books on social media!

FURTHER READING

BIBLIOGRAPHY

- Citizens Advice. (No date) *Harassment at work*. [Online]. [Accessed 12 October 2017]. Available from: <https://www.citizensadvice.org.uk/work/discrimination-at-work/what-are-the-different-types-of-discrimination/harassment-at-work/>

- Gava, M-J. (2007) *Harcèlement moral : comment s'en sortir ?* Paris: Prat Éditions.

- Gov.uk. (No date) *Dismissal: your rights*. [Online]. [Accessed 12 October 2017]. Available from: <https://www.gov.uk/dismissal/unfair-and-constructive-dismissal>

- Gov.uk. (No date) *Workplace bullying and harassment*. [Online]. [Accessed 12 October 2017]. Available from: <https://www.gov.uk/workplace-bullying-and-harassment>

- Hirigoyen, M-F. (1998) *Le harcèlement moral : la violence perverse au quotidien*. Paris: La Découverte.

- Laundau, P. (2017) Bullying at work: your legal rights. *The Guardian*. [Online]. [Accessed 12 October 2017]. Available from: <https://www.theguardian.com/careers/2017/mar/29/>

• bullying-at-work-your-legal-rights>

• (2002) *Le harcèlement moral au travail : nouveau terrain d'action syndicale.* Brussels: Centre national des employés.

• (2006) *On ne joue pas avec le harcèlement !* Brussels: Confédération des syndicats chrétiens.

• Rulkin, D. (No date) Le harcèlement moral au travail. *LePsychologue.be.* [Online]. [Accessed 12 October 2017]. Available from: <https://www.lepsychologue.be/articles/harcelement-moral.php>

ADDITIONAL SOURCES

• Adams, A. (1992) *Bullying At Work: How to Confront and Overcome It.* London: Virago.

• Clifford, L. (2006) *Survive Bullying at Work.* London: A & C Black Publishers Ltd.

• Peyton, P. R. (2003) *Dignity at Work: Eliminate Bullying and Create a Positive Working Environment.* Hove: Routledge.

www.50minutes.com

Ebook EAN: 9782808000376

Paperback EAN: 9782808000383

Legal Deposit: D/2017/12603/446

Cover: © Primento

Digital conception by Primento, the digital partner of publishers.